AF725786

MAHLIA AMATINA

Autism and Work

Copyright © 2026 by Mahlia Amatina

All rights reserved. No part of this publication may be reproduced, stored, or transmitted in any form or by any means, electronic, mechanical, photocopying, recording, scanning, or otherwise without written permission from the publisher. It is illegal to copy this book, post it to a website, or distribute it by any other means without permission.

Mahlia Amatina asserts the moral right to be identified as the author of this work.

Mahlia Amatina has no responsibility for the persistence or accuracy of URLs for external or third-party Internet Websites referred to in this publication and does not guarantee that any content on such Websites is, or will remain, accurate or appropriate.

The content of this book is provided for educational and informational purposes only. While every effort has been made to ensure accuracy, the author makes no warranties, express or implied, regarding the completeness, reliability or suitability of the material.

To protect the privacy of individuals featured in case studies and stories, names and identifying details have been slightly amended. Any resemblance to actual persons, living or deceased, is purely coincidental.

This book does not constitute legal, medical, financial or other professional advice. Readers should consult qualified professionals before making decisions based on the content herein.

These terms shall be governed by and construed in accordance with the laws of England and Wales. Any dispute arising under or in connection with this book shall be subject to the exclusive jurisdiction of the courts of England and Wales.

First edition

ISBN: 978-1-9195538-0-1

Editing by Grace Gilbert
Cover art by Erin Caitlin Karn (using licensed Canva elements)

This book was professionally typeset on Reedsy.
Find out more at reedsy.com

Contents

1

Introduction: Why This Book Matters

Autistic individuals can often face unique and complex challenges in the workplace that can make employment difficult, despite having incredible strengths to offer. I created this book to empower you with practical strategies, compassionate insights and firsthand experiences that illuminate a path, not just to survive at work, but to thrive: because we deserve to.

This book is rooted in both lived experience and professional exploration. As an autistic person, I've spent years navigating work environments that weren't designed with neurodivergent brains in mind. I've written extensively on these topics through my blog at www.mahliaamatina.com, where I share personal stories, workplace reflections and tips for both autistic individuals and inclusive employers. On my Instagram, *@mahliaamatina*, I openly explore themes of mental health, autistic identity, sensory cognition and the intersections of autism with creativity and wellbeing.

Through art and advocacy, I've connected with countless individuals who share similar struggles, navigating burnout, sensory overload, miscommunication and barriers to access, while also holding incredible potential, creativity and depth. Too often, autistic professionals are expected to mould themselves to systems that don't accommodate our needs. This book challenges that expectation.

Instead of prescribing one-size-fits-all solutions, this guide is an invitation to reflect, adapt and advocate for environments where you can truly succeed. Whether you're newly diagnosed, self-identifying or years into your autistic journey, I hope this book helps you feel seen, supported and empowered to take your next steps on your terms.

2

Understanding the Autistic Profile at Work

The concept of the “spiky profile” is a valuable way to understand how autistic individuals can possess exceptional strengths in certain areas while facing significant challenges in others. Rather than viewing abilities on a flat, linear spectrum, the spiky profile recognises that skills, sensitivities and responses can vary dramatically, even within the same person. You might excel in pattern recognition, attention to detail or creativity, yet find yourself overwhelmed by ambiguous instructions, sensory input or rapid social interactions.

In the workplace, this can mean being a top performer in one aspect of a role, while struggling silently with another. For example, an autistic employee may produce outstanding reports or innovate solutions, yet be completely drained by open-plan office noise, spontaneous meetings or unclear expectations. These uneven spikes of ability are not flaws; they’re simply features of how autistic minds work.

Recognising and accepting this spiky profile is an empowering step. It allows you to holistically understand your needs, advocate for adjustments and build environments that support (not suppress) your authenticity. As I share in my blog, the spiky profile reminds us that we are not “less than” for having limitations. We are wired differently, and when supported appropriately, we can thrive.

Alongside this, many autistic people also experience co-occurring conditions like anxiety, depression or other neurodivergent conditions, like ADHD. These are often intensified by external pressures to mask, perform or conform. Understanding your profile means acknowledging both your challenges and your capacity, so you can move toward roles and routines that align with your energy and strengths.

In my experience and that of others I've spoken to, embracing your profile can be life changing. It shifts the focus from "fixing" yourself to honouring your needs. Whether that means more structured communication, sensory-friendly workspaces or a flexible schedule, it starts with self-awareness. When you know yourself deeply, you're in a stronger position to ask for what you need and create a working life that nurtures, rather than depletes you.

3

Navigating Sensory and Environmental Triggers

Bright lights, open-plan offices, background noise, strong smells and unexpected interruptions can all act as sensory triggers. These environmental factors can overwhelm the senses of autistic individuals and lead to intense physical and emotional reactions, such as shutdowns, meltdowns, fatigue or difficulty concentrating.

These reactions are not overreactions; they're protective responses from a nervous system that processes information differently. What might be a minor distraction to a neurotypical colleague, like a flickering light or the buzz of a printer, can be deeply distressing and disruptive to someone who is autistic.

From my own experience and conversations with other autistic individuals, I've learned that sensory overload can become cumulative. Small environmental discomforts layered throughout the day increase anxiety and reduce productivity, ultimately leading to burnout. This is why recognising your triggers early and having practical responses in place is essential.

Common triggers include:

- Harsh, fluorescent or flickering lighting
- Overpowering smells (perfume, food, cleaning products)
- Loud conversations or phones ringing
- Inconsistent temperatures
- Visual clutter or constant movement in the periphery

Practical strategies that can help mitigate these include:

- Wearing noise-cancelling headphones or ear defenders
- Requesting a desk in a quieter area or using desk dividers
- Asking for adjustments to lighting or using natural light where possible
- Taking regular sensory breaks to decompress in a quiet space
- Working from home, either full-time or part-time

If you feel safe to do so, advocating for these accommodations with your employer can make a world of difference. It's often helpful to frame these requests not just in terms of what you need, but in how they will support your performance and wellbeing.

You might say: "I've noticed that I work much more effectively in a space with lower lighting and fewer interruptions. Would it be possible to use a desk lamp instead of overhead lighting, and relocate to a quieter area?"

Many autistic people find that even one or two targeted adjustments can drastically reduce sensory overwhelm. Remember, your needs are not too much. Truly. They are legitimate, and creating a manageable sensory environment is not a luxury; it's a necessity for sustainable work.

You are the expert on your own sensory world, and the more you learn about what supports or hinders your nervous system, the more equipped you'll be to design a workplace experience that truly allows you to succeed.

4

Preventing Autistic Burnout

Autistic burnout is real, and it's not just about being tired. It's a state of chronic mental, emotional and physical exhaustion caused by prolonged masking, sensory overload or unrealistic expectations. It often builds slowly, and by the time it's recognised it can be deeply debilitating.

Many autistic people describe burnout as a sense of complete depletion, where once-manageable tasks feel insurmountable, and even basic functioning becomes a struggle. You might experience memory loss, increased sensitivity, disassociation or emotional shutdown. Unlike typical burnout, autistic burnout is often the result of years of having to suppress your natural responses in order to fit in or cope with environments that aren't designed for neurodivergent minds.

In my blog, I've written about how burnout creeps in when you are constantly pushing through discomfort, masking your identity or absorbing the pressure to perform without adequate rest or understanding. It can feel like trying to keep up with a world that doesn't pause to accommodate your needs and never learning how to say stop.

Preventing burnout starts with identifying your early warning signs.

These might include:

- Feeling more fatigued than usual, even after sleep
- Avoiding social contact or dreading work-related communication
- Becoming more sensitive to sensory inputs or stressors
- Losing motivation or focus
- Feeling detached or emotionally numb

Once you begin to recognise your patterns, you can put proactive strategies in place. These may include:

- Scheduling regular breaks throughout the day - even short pauses to breathe or decompress
- Building rest and downtime into your weekly routine as a non-negotiable
- Creating firm boundaries around your time and energy
- Reducing masking by allowing yourself to stim, communicate authentically or say no when needed
- Seeking out environments and roles that allow you to work with your flow, not against it

It can be helpful to work with a therapist or coach who understands neurodiversity, especially if you're trying to unlearn internalised expectations of productivity or perfectionism. And if you're in burnout now, please give yourself permission to pause. Recovery might mean stepping away from work altogether for a period, and that's okay. Rest is not laziness; it's a radical act of self-preservation.

Workplaces also need to play their part. Employers must learn to recognise the signs of burnout in their neurodivergent staff and build supportive structures around pacing, flexibility and communication. Prevention is not the sole responsibility of the individual.

Ultimately, preventing burnout is about self-awareness, self-compassion and creating a life that allows you to live in alignment with who you are: not who you feel pressured to be. Self-care isn't a luxury; it's essential maintenance, and self-knowledge is your greatest tool. With this, you can begin to reclaim your energy, your joy and your space in the workplace on your own terms.

5

Disclosure and Reasonable Adjustments

Deciding whether to disclose your diagnosis at work is deeply personal. For many autistic individuals, it can feel risky or vulnerable, especially in environments where neurodiversity is not well understood. There is no universal right answer, only the one that feels right for you in your specific context and stage of life.

In my experience, I've faced moments when disclosing my diagnosis felt essential for survival. One such moment came during a period of deep burnout, where continuing to mask my challenges was no longer an option. I was experiencing sensory overwhelm, anxiety and exhaustion every day, and I knew that unless something changed, I would have to leave the workplace altogether. When I finally disclosed my diagnosis, I was met with a mix of responses, some positive, some hesitant, but it opened the door to important conversations and crucial adjustments.

You are legally entitled in Great Britain to request reasonable adjustments under the Equality Act 2010, with or without disclosure. These adjustments are designed to level the playing field, not to offer unfair advantage. You are not asking for special treatment; you are asserting your right to fair access with changes to activities that have a long-term negative effect on your day-to-day living.

Examples of reasonable adjustments include:

- Written rather than verbal instructions
- Extra time for tasks or preparation
- A buddy or mentor for onboarding and transitions
- Clear agendas and expectations for meetings
- Quiet or low-stimulation workspaces
- Flexible working hours or remote work

It helps to be as specific as possible about what you may need and why. For instance, rather than saying "I get overwhelmed easily," you might say: "I focus best in low-noise environments and would benefit from noise-cancelling headphones and a seat away from the main people-traffic area."

You can also frame adjustments around how they benefit the wider workplace, enhancing productivity, communication and wellbeing for all. Many adjustments for autistic employees turn out to be "universally designed" strategies that help everyone, and any decent employer will recognise this.

In one job, I found it helpful to create a short document that explained my working style, strengths and what support I needed. This gave my manager clarity and also took the pressure off me to verbally explain things every time a new challenge arose. In another role, I advocated for a phased return after time off, which helped me re-engage at a manageable pace.

Not every workplace will be immediately responsive. Unfortunately, some may still hold biases or lack awareness. If this happens, know that you are not alone. You can seek support through HR, occupational health or external services such as Access to Work, which can offer assessments and funding for adjustments.

Ultimately, disclosure is not a one-time decision; you may choose to share parts of your experience gradually, or only with trusted colleagues. You get to decide what, when and how much to share.

Whether you choose to disclose or not, your needs are valid. You deserve to work in an environment that honours who you are. With the right adjustments, thriving becomes not just possible, but sustainable.

6

Social Navigation and Communication

Workplaces often prize social fluidity, spontaneity, and an unwritten understanding of office etiquette, which can feel confusing or exhausting for many autistic individuals. These "soft skills" often involve reading between the lines, deciphering tone of voice or navigating group dynamics; all areas where autistic people may experience challenges. From my own experience, I've found social navigation at work to be one of the most misunderstood aspects of autism. In past roles, I've been perceived as quiet, distant or "too direct," when in reality I was simply trying to process the environment, understand the task and communicate clearly. These misunderstandings can lead to exclusion, miscommunication or a lack of trust, even when the work itself is excellent.

A common scenario is being left out of informal chats or decisions made "off the record" in break rooms or over lunch. Because so much social bonding happens in unstructured, spontaneous ways, autistic people can inadvertently be sidelined from important relationship-building or networking opportunities.

This is where structure can be your best friend. Scheduled check-ins, clear agendas, written follow-ups and a preference for email over phone calls are not just quirks; they are access tools that enable you to participate on your terms. These tools reduce ambiguity and cognitive overload, and they also create transparency, which helps avoid confusion.

If you're someone who prefers written over verbal communication, it's worth letting colleagues know this early on. For example, you could say: "I find I communicate most clearly in writing, do you mind if I follow up our meeting with a quick summary email?" Framing these preferences around clarity and mutual understanding can help build trust.

Many workplaces are now forming neurodiversity networks or peer-support groups, which can be a great way to connect with others who share similar challenges. Buddy systems can also offer a low-pressure way to build relationships with one or two colleagues who understand your communication style.

Autistic people often thrive in environments where communication is direct, kind and predictable. That doesn't mean you can't engage in social relationships; it just means you might do so in your own way, with your own rhythm.

And remember, communication isn't just about words. Many autistic people are deeply empathetic, thoughtful and observant, qualities that are invaluable in team dynamics. Just because your communication doesn't fit the norm doesn't mean it isn't effective.

You don't have to change who you are to succeed. You simply need a workplace culture and communication methods that honour and uplift your natural ways of connecting.

7

Recruitment and Alternative Pathways

Traditional recruitment processes can be inaccessible for many autistic individuals. The reliance on vague job descriptions, open-ended interviews and unspoken social rules can make it difficult for neurodivergent candidates to show their true potential. Standard interviews often reward quick thinking, confident eye contact and small talk, none of which are necessarily indicators of job performance, and many of which can pose challenges for autistic people.

In my blog, I've written about how these barriers create a disconnect between talent and opportunity. When I applied for roles in the past, I often found the process more about navigating ambiguity and reading hidden cues than about my actual ability to do the work. This left me frustrated and disheartened, especially knowing I had so much to offer (creativity, focus, dedication) if only I were given a fair chance to demonstrate it.

Fortunately, alternative recruitment models are gaining traction. These include:

- **Portfolio-based applications:** allowing candidates to showcase what they can do, rather than talk about it hypothetically.

- **Skills-based assessments:** practical tasks that reflect real job responsibilities, offering a more accurate gauge of suitability.
- **Advance sharing of interview questions:** giving candidates time to prepare and reduce anxiety.
- **Flexible interview formats:** offering video submissions, written responses or alternative ways to communicate.
- **Trial shifts or job previews:** letting people experience the role in action before making a formal commitment.

As someone who works in both creative and advocacy spaces, I've seen firsthand how autistic individuals flourish when given autonomy and flexibility. Many find joy and success in self-employment, freelancing or entrepreneurial ventures that allow them to design their own workflows and honour their energy levels. For me, developing a portfolio career has allowed me to craft a professional life that plays to my strengths and accommodates my needs.

If traditional employment models haven't worked for you, know that you're not alone and that doesn't mean you're unemployable. Far from. It means the system wasn't designed for you. That's why so many autistic people are exploring alternative pathways, including:

- Remote or hybrid roles
- Part-time or project-based contracts
- Creative or craft-based work
- Advocacy, education or peer support
- Setting up their own business or collective

The key is alignment: finding work that fits your values, interests and sensory profile. That might mean redefining what success looks like or stepping away from conventional expectations. Your worth isn't determined by a CV or how you come across in an interview. Your value lies in who you are and what you bring, and there are many ways to make that shine.

The goal is not just to get a job. It's to find work that works *for you.* And when that happens, thriving becomes not only possible, but inevitable.

8

Managing Mental Health at Work

Depression and anxiety are common co-occurring conditions with autism; managing them within the demands of a workplace can feel like an uphill battle, especially in environments where mental health is still stigmatised or misunderstood.

For many autistic individuals, mental health challenges aren't just occasional; they can be chronic and cyclical, often exacerbated by sensory overload, social misunderstandings, lack of routine or the effort of masking. In my writing, I've shared how this interplay between autism and mental health can sometimes feel like a constant balancing act. Even when things seem fine on the surface, the emotional and cognitive load underneath can be immense.

One of the most powerful things I've learned is the importance of listening to your early warning signs. For me, it might start with difficulty waking up in the morning, a feeling of numbness or detachment, or a sense of dread about even small tasks. Left unacknowledged, these can spiral into periods of burnout or deep depression.

Some strategies that have helped me, and others in the community, include:

- **Taking mental health days:** rest is essential. If your body and mind are telling you they need to pause, honour that.
- **Therapy and counselling:** especially with practitioners who understand neurodivergence. Having a space where you don't need to mask can be deeply healing.
- **Phased returns after time off:** if you've been unwell, don't rush back. A gradual reintegration into work can support long-term stability.
- **Peer support networks:** talking with others who "get it" helps reduce isolation and normalise your experience. Sometimes just being seen and validated is enough to make a hard day feel manageable.
- **Structuring your week:** I've found that building in regular 'rest windows' throughout my week, like protected mornings or sensory recovery breaks, prevents overload before it starts.

It's also important to create emotional safety in your environment, which might mean:

- Setting boundaries with colleagues or managers around communication styles
- Clearly scheduling downtime and non-negotiable breaks
- Keeping a journal to track mood, energy and workload
- Advocating for autonomy where possible, as autistic people often thrive with control over their time and environment

Some workplaces are beginning to recognise the link between mental health and neurodiversity. If your employer has an employee assistance programme (EAP), it may offer free therapy sessions or wellbeing resources. Don't be afraid to ask what supports exist, and advocate for those that don't yet.

You do not need to push through in silence. Seeking help is not a weakness; it's an act of strength. You are allowed to ask for support. You are allowed to rest. And you are allowed to exist in your workplace as your whole self: mental health needs and all.

Managing mental health at work is not just about coping, it's about creating conditions where you can thrive emotionally, socially and professionally. It starts with self-compassion and continues with systems of support that centre your wellbeing.

You are not alone, and you do not need to push through in silence.

9

Building Community and Support Networks

Having others who "get it" can be transformative. Whether through workplace initiatives, online spaces or community-led events, finding your neurotribe (those who understand your experience intuitively) can offer a powerful sense of belonging and validation.

In my own journey, building community has been one of the most affirming parts of navigating life as an autistic professional. When I first started writing publicly about autism and work, I didn't anticipate the number of people who would reach out with similar stories: of burnout, of masking, of being misunderstood or overlooked. These exchanges reminded me that I wasn't alone, and they opened the door to deeper conversations and mutual support.

Support doesn't always need to come from within your immediate team or employer. In fact, some of the most meaningful connections I've made have come from external neurodiversity networks, social media platforms like Instagram and in-person meetups or advocacy collectives. These spaces have allowed me to share authentically, exchange advice and build friendships rooted in shared experience.

Here are some ways to build your own support networks:

- **Join neurodivergent affinity or employee resource groups** at work (or start one if it doesn't exist).
- **Connect via social media**, following hashtags like #ActuallyAutistic or #NeurodivergentAtWork.
- **Attend autism-focused conferences, workshops or events** such as Autistica projects, Annual Professionals' Conference or The Autism & ADHD Show.
- **Participate in online forums** like Wrong Planet, Reddit's r/autism and Facebook or Discord groups for autistic adults.
- **Join communities** like Neurodiversity in Business to connect through shared identity and purpose.

You can also seek out a mentor: someone who has lived experience of autism in the workplace and can offer guidance. Or you can become that person for someone else. Sharing your story can be an act of connection and empowerment, and you never know who might find courage or clarity through your words.

In one of my blog posts, I wrote about how isolating work can feel when you're masking your needs day after day. But I also shared how a single conversation with another autistic colleague gave me the strength to ask for adjustments, and reminded me that support was possible. It doesn't take a large network to make a difference. Even one ally can change the trajectory of your experience.

Support networks can offer:

- A safe space to vent or problem-solve
- Practical strategies that others have tried
- Emotional validation and solidarity
- Opportunities to advocate collectively for change

These relationships create buffers against the strain of navigating inaccessible systems on your own. They offer reminders that your struggles are not personal failures, but reflections of broader systemic gaps.

And finally, building community isn't just about support, it's about joy. Sharing laughter, creativity and celebration with people who embrace you as you are is deeply healing. Work can be a space not just of challenge, but of connection. And those connections can light the way forward.

So, whether online or offline, through work or beyond it, keep seeking your people. They're out there, and they're looking for you too.

10

Your Rights and Employer Responsibilities

Understanding your legal rights is an essential part of building confidence and resilience in the workplace. In Great Britain, autistic individuals are protected under the Equality Act 2010, which defines disability as a physical or mental impairment that has a substantial and long-term adverse effect on a person's ability to carry out normal day-to-day activities. Autism qualifies under this definition, whether or not you have a formal diagnosis.

Key Rights under the Equality Act 2010

- **Protection from Discrimination:** employers cannot treat you unfairly or less favourably because of your autism. This includes during recruitment, training, promotion, dismissal or any other part of employment.
- **Reasonable Adjustments:** employers have a legal duty to make reasonable adjustments to reduce or remove any disadvantages you may face due to your autism. These adjustments aim to create equity, not privilege.
- **Protection from Harassment and Victimisation:** the law also

protects you from bullying or retaliation for asserting your rights or making a complaint.

Reasonable adjustments are tailored to the individual and might include:

- Flexible start and end times
- A quieter workstation or remote working
- Written rather than verbal instructions
- Advance notice of meetings and changes
- Providing interview questions in advance

Employers are expected to anticipate and accommodate the needs of disabled employees, not to wait for crises to occur before acting. If you disclose your autism, they are then legally obligated to consider what adjustments would be reasonable to ensure your success and wellbeing.

Access to Work

One powerful support available in Great Britain is the Access to Work scheme. This government-funded programme provides financial support for practical workplace adjustments, including:

- Specialist equipment
- Job coaching
- Support workers or interpreters
- Mental health support

You can apply for Access to Work independently, and it's worth doing even if your employer isn't familiar with it. More info: www.gov.uk/access-to-work

What to Do If Your Rights Are Not Respected

If you face discrimination or your employer fails to make reasonable adjustments:

- Raise the issue informally first, with your line manager or HR
- If necessary, follow the company's formal grievance procedure
- Seek advice from ACAS (Advisory, Conciliation and Arbitration Service) at www.acas.org.uk
- Contact organisations such as Citizens Advice, Equality Advisory Support Service (EASS), or an autism charity like the National Autistic Society

You are not alone, and you have legal protections in place for a reason. It is not "making a fuss" to ask for what you need; it is your *right.*

Too often, we are made to feel as though we are the problem. But the problem is rarely the individual; it's the system that hasn't adapted. Knowing your rights empowers you to take up space with confidence, to advocate without guilt and to insist on being treated with fairness and dignity.

You deserve a workplace that supports your whole self. When you know your rights, you can begin to build not only a job that works for you, but a future that honours your strengths, protects your wellbeing and upholds your worth. You are entitled to reasonable adjustments if you have a disability, including autism.

Employers are legally required to ensure you are not at a disadvantage because of your diagnosis. If you're unsure of your rights, organisations like ACAS, Access to Work or autism charities can provide guidance.

Knowledge is power, and knowing your rights gives you a solid foundation to advocate for yourself.

11

Conclusion: Thriving is Possible

Thriving at work as an autistic individual is not a distant dream; it is a real, tangible possibility. But to get there, we must first shift the narrative from one of mere survival to one of empowerment, pride and belonging. This book offered reflections, strategies and personal stories with one core message at its heart: you deserve to be here, and you have so much to offer.

You are not too much. You are not too sensitive, too direct, too different or too complicated. You are uniquely you, and with that comes a wealth of creativity, focus, empathy and insight. These are not deficits to be managed, but gifts to be recognised, nurtured and celebrated.

Through my own journey, I've learned that work doesn't have to be something that demolishes us. It can be a space for growth, expression and contribution. But that only happens when we are allowed to show up fully as ourselves. Whether you're advocating for reasonable adjustments, seeking community, managing mental health or redefining success on your own terms, remember that you are not alone: your path matters.

To my fellow autistic professionals reading this: your presence in the workplace is not just valid, it is vital. You have the right to ask for what you need. You have the right to take up space. And you have the right to thrive; not in spite of your autism, but because of the richness it brings to your work and your world.

I hope this book has helped you feel more seen, more equipped and more hopeful. Keep connecting, keep creating and keep claiming your place. The workplace needs your voice, your vision and your truth. And above all, never forget you are enough, exactly as you are.

About the Author

Mahlia Amatina is an award-winning neurodivergent author, artist and advocate, passionate about creativity, inclusion and reimagining the workplace. Diagnosed as autistic in adulthood and named one of the *Top 50 Influential Neurodiverse Women,* by Women Beyond the Box, Mahlia brings both lived experience and professional insight to her work, bridging the gap between theory, research and the day-to-day realities of autistic life.

Join Mahlia's online community and never miss a new project:

You can connect with me on:

- https://www.mahliaamatina.com
- https://www.facebook.com/MahliaAmatina
- https://linktr.ee/MahliaAmatina
- https://www.instagram.com/MahliaAmatina

Also by Mahlia Amatina

If this book spoke to you, please take a moment to leave a review:

- On your reading platform
- On Goodreads, search "Mahlia Amatina" to find her author page
- Directly on Mahlia's website via the contact form

Your feedback helps Mahlia reach more readers and continue advocating for inclusivity within the workplace. Thank you!

Creative Rest: An Artful Toolkit for Autistic Overwhelm

Gentle exercises and heartfelt guidance to help you find peace, clarity and joy through creativity.

In a world that rarely slows down, autistic minds often carry the weight of sensory overload, social pressure and emotional intensity. Rest can feel unreachable or misunderstood. This book invites you to discover a different kind of rest: one that's creative, compassionate and deeply healing.

Through accessible art exercises, reflective journalling prompts and nurturing self-care strategies, *Creative Rest* offers a gentle path back to yourself. Whether you're navigating overwhelm, shutdown or emotional fatigue, this toolkit will help you regulate your feelings, reconnect with your inner world and honour your unique needs with kindness.

There is no "right" way to rest creatively: only your way. This book is your safe space to explore, express and renew at your own pace, reminding you that rest isn't a luxury but a vital act of self-love.

Dear Manager: How to Support Your Autistic Employees

Unlock the potential of autistic talent - and transform your workplace.

Written by an autistic professional, *Dear Manager: How to Support Your Autistic Employees* blends lived experience, cutting-edge research and practical strategies to help managers and HR teams create truly inclusive environments. Covering everything from reasonable adjustments and sensory needs to the role of intersectionality in shaping experiences, this is your essential guide to helping autistic employees not just survive, but thrive.

Autistic Burnout and Mental Health at Work

Feeling drained, overwhelmed or on the edge of burnout? For autistic professionals, burnout isn't just stress: it's survival.

In *Autistic Burnout & Mental Health at Work*, Mahlia Amatina combines lived experience, research and practical tools to help you:

Recognise the early signs of autistic burnout

Recover with phased returns, sensory restoration and energy pacing

Request reasonable adjustments and Access to Work support

Build sustainable wellbeing and belonging at work

Whether you're autistic, supporting an autistic colleague or creating an inclusive workplace, this book offers clarity, compassion and strategies you can use right away.

You are not broken. You are worthy of rest, support and a working life that lets you thrive.

The Autistic Employee Workplace Toolkit

Practical Strategies for Thriving at Work - Self-Advocacy, Sensory Overload Management, Reasonable Adjustments and Career Growth for Autistic Professionals.

Thrive as an autistic professional with this practical, empowering guide. Packed with strategies for workplace accommodations, reasonable adjustments, managing sensory overload and self-advocacy, this toolkit helps you navigate autism in the workplace with confidence. Discover how to protect your emotional wellbeing, set clear boundaries, prevent autistic burnout and build a sustainable, fulfilling career.

www.ingramcontent.com/pod-product-compliance
Lightning Source LLC
LaVergne TN
LVHW090336210926
848480LV00004B/1437
9781919553801